I Found Out How Babies Are Made!

CW01619252

By D. F. Zaman

Copyright ©2024 *D. F. Zaman*

All rights reserved

Acknowledgements

In loving memory of my mother, Saleha Barlasker, who raised me as a single parent. She did the best she could for me under difficult circumstances and for that, I am forever grateful.

Special thanks to Vajihe Golmazari, Cover Illustrator.

Foreword by the Author

I wrote this book as a tribute to my mother after she passed away on 29th April 2023.

My God fearing, devout mother had raised me as a single parent and had taught me that being good, working hard and following the rules would lead to a better life.

It didn't.

Living in a gang-infested, crime-infested city, I lost nearly three decades of my life to crime in an environment where people lie, cheat, steal and commit covert acts of violence casually.

Sadly, we are living in a time when some people are morally bankrupt and will lie for various reasons such as jealousy, tribal vendettas and bribes.

Some of the wealthiest people in the world today (Illuminati) are the most morally bankrupt and corrupt people in the world. These trillionaires can bribe hundreds of people to commit crimes and to tell lies. We even went to war on lies and a million people lost their lives. People have been killed on lies.

When someone finds themselves a target for very wealthy, morally bankrupt criminals, their lives are never the same again.

I found myself a target for such criminals because of a parent who had been out of my life from the time that I was TEN years old, someone who had moved on and had a second family and had done nothing for me after the age of TEN.

This was a parent who never paid child support or even sent a birthday card.

A child without a father lacks a protector and a provider and is therefore, a child who has less.

My aim in writing this book is to honour my mother for all that she did for me as a single parent and to make a very serious point, that single parents and their children can have less than families with two parents.

According to an article in the Guardian of 4th July 2022, half of all children in single parent families live in relative poverty.

> **It is important that those who were fatherless and deprived as children are NOT deprived all over again because of crime or because of Anti-Christ/Luciferian/ Satanic bribery and corruption leading to a culture of casual lies.**

Only someone sleep-walking through life today would fail to notice the countless celebrities in well-paid industries, e.g. the music industry, movie industry and sports who are engaging in bizarre behaviours such as making pyramid signs and other odd behaviours in order to pay homage to the order of the Illuminati which is a Luciferian/ anti-Christ organisation with many members across the globe.

We are living in dangerous times where some of the richest and most powerful people in the world are the most immoral and are corrupting society from the top down.

The Anti-Christ criminal with trillions in the bank cares NOTHING for Christian values or wider Abrahamic values that teach us to care for those who are less fortunate or fatherless but hopefully, decent people WILL care.

I hope that this book helps people to understand the plight of single parent families and the very real hardships that some of these families can face.

It is terrifying for someone who grew up in a single parent home and had less to find themselves a target for sinister Satanic/ Luciferian oligarchs, bereft of moral values with trillions in the bank, who misuse that money to bribe people to lie in great numbers about the person who had less in order to deprive them all over again.

That is why it is important for people to inform targets of defamation what is being said behind their back and by whom so that targeted individuals can take legal action and defend their rights.

Single parents and their children can have lives that are tough as this largely autobiographical story shows.

My mother and I suffered terribly because of gossip culture which facilitates backstabbing and abuse.

In writing this book, I hope that no single parent family will ever suffer again as my mother and I have suffered.

Chapter One- My Mum's Not Like That!

Have you ever had a day that left you gob-smacked, that turned your whole world upside down?

Well that day was today for me because today was the day that I found out how babies are made!

Sarah and Austin told me in the school playground.

I didn't believe it at first. I shook my head and said,

"No! MY mum would NEVER do THAT!"

But they laughed and said,

"She did! She did!"

I still refused to believe it.

I said, *"My mum's not like that. She'd NEVER do anything like that and if she did, she'd TELL me!"*

And then, I thought, *"WOULD she tell me?"*

And that's when I knew it was true.

I thought to myself, *"If that's how they make babies, that means my mum's done it. Mrs Thatcher's done it... AND... THE QUEEN! They've all been doing things with their bits, the grown-ups!"*

Then, as if that wasn't bad enough, just a week later, I found out something else that's weird about grown-ups. Some of them PEE in the street!

It happened when I was over at a friend's house. I've been friends with Delina ever since I can remember, ever since I was born. There's a photo in our album of two mothers in the park with their babies. I'm the new-born baby in my mother's arms as she glares grumpily at the camera, looking as if she hasn't slept in ages and Delina's there in her mother's arms, a two-year-old toddler, holding a packet of Jelly Tots, looking really pleased with herself.

Well, fast forward ten years to 1982, and picture Delina standing by her window, a look of HORROR on her face! She's beckoning me to come and look out the window and have a look at the horrible thing that's happening.

"Dani! Get over here NOW! Come and have a look at THIS!"

So, I rushed over to the window and guess what? Guess what I saw? I saw a GROWN-UP, peeing in the street!!!

Can you believe it?

This week has been a SERIOUSLY weird week. I would say that it has been life-changing.

All my life, I thought that grown-ups were perfect, that grown-ups could do no wrong.

I used to feel like a VIP if one of the dinner ladies held my hand in the school playground or when she patted me on the head and told me I was a "good girl," for handing in a piece of glass I'd found in the playground. It meant so much to me back then because back when we were little, we thought that grown- ups were gods!

Now, I realise that they do weird things with their bits to make babies and that some of them PEE in the street!

Chapter Two- Miss Ellis

The next day at school, I kept looking at my teacher, Miss Ellis to try and work out if she had ever done IT. The thing about Miss Ellis is that she looks normal. She doesn't look like someone who does things with her bits! I kept staring and staring and staring at her, looking for a sign that she had but she looks normal.

I kept thinking, *"Miss Ellis, are you one of THEM Miss Ellis? Have you done things with your bits? Miss Ellis? MISS ELLIS?"* But no matter how long I stared at her, I couldn't see anything wrong with her! She looks normal just like my mother!

Well, she doesn't look exactly like my mother. Miss Ellis is my main teacher in my last of year primary school and she's really pretty whereas my mum looks... well...like... a mum.

Miss Ellis is about twenty five. She has big, blue eyes, honey blond hair to her shoulders and the most warm, beautiful smile. I think she could have been a supermodel but she's a teacher like my mother.

You know, the more I think of it, the less I can imagine Miss Ellis doing IT. She doesn't seem the type. She's so… normal.

Then again, so is my mum. So is Mrs Thatcher and so is the queen but they've all been doing things with their bits because they've all had babies!

You know, I don't understand grown-ups. I really don't! I mean, how can you do THAT and be normal?

Chapter Three- The Baby Thief

When I got home after Sarah and Austin told me how babies are made, I looked at my mother in a new way too.

It was all very different back in 1975 when I was three. Back then, I thought that all babies were made in hospitals by the doctors and nurses who worked in the hospitals and that you could go in and buy one like a kitten or a puppy! I thought it was THAT easy!

I loved babies and I was desperate for a baby brother or sister to play with, so every time we walked past the local hospital, I would make my mother's life a misery, insisting that she go in and get me a baby *"NOW!"*

Every time Mum and I walked past South London Women's Hospital, my mother and I would have a tug of war!

I would be there in front of the hospital, tugging at my mother's hand, pulling her towards the hospital, begging,

"Mummy! Please! Let's go in a get a baby! I want a baby brother or sister to play with. Let's go in and get a baby NOW......PLEEEZE!"

I was desperate to have a baby brother or sister because I hated being an only child.

My mother would end up all hot and bothered, trying to rein me in and she'd reply,

"Not today Danita. Another day maybe. Not today. We're busy. Tomorrow, OK? Maybe tomorrow."

But tomorrow never came.

Then, there was Delina, my mother's friend's daughter who was five. She was competing with me over whose mother loved them more and whose mother was going to give them a baby brother or sister!

We'd have these silly conversations that little children have.

She'd say, *"I bet my mummy gets me a baby before YOUR mummy gets you a baby because MY mummy loves me more!"*

And I'd say, *"No, I bet MY mummy gets me a baby before your mummy gets you a baby because MY mummy loves ME more!"*

And she'd reply, *"No, MY mummy!"*

And I'd insist, *"No, MY mummy!"* and then, I'd stick out my tongue out at her!

Really clever stuff. Then again, in our defence, we were only three and five at the time!

Then, one day, Delina's mum came over to our house and she told me something amazing. She told me that there was a baby on the way and what's more, she laughed and she said that I could have it!

Well, when a grown up tells you something, you believe it when you're three so I thought that they were making a baby at the hospital just for me!

So, day after day, I reminded my mother to make sure that we got to the hospital first when the baby was ready to leave so that Delina couldn't get there first and take the baby that they were making at the hospital for me!

My mother used to nod and smile when I used to remind her, so I was sure that I was about to get a baby sister or brother until the day my hopes were dashed cruelly.

It happened when I overheard my mother saying to my father,

"Delina and her dad are going to the hospital. It's a boy."

And that's when I knew that my mother had betrayed me. She had gone and given Delina my baby! She loved Delina more than me!

I went ballistic.

My mother turned around to see my jaw drop, my eyes widen as I took in what had just happened and then, the screaming started and it went on and on for hours, she told me.

I screamed at my mother, saying, *"Delina's mummy's a good mummy. She gave her a baby. You don't give me ANYTHING!"* which wasn't strictly true as my mum did get me books and toys and things but I wanted something living and breathing to love and take care of and play with.

All hopes dashed, I sat in my cot and cried for hours, tears streaming down my face.

I couldn't understand why my mother wouldn't give me a baby brother or sister to play with despite all the begging and the pleading. I thought it was because she didn't love me.

It would be years before I realised that my mother didn't want any more children because she was unhappy in her marriage and she was planning to leave my father someday when I was older.

But when I was four, I didn't know that. I just thought to myself, *"My mummy doesn't love me. Delina's mummy loves her more,"* and so, I cried bitter tears.

Chapter Four– She Can't Have My Ribena!

It was around the time that Delina got her baby brother that I began to think of my mother as a traitor.

Not only had she let Delina steal my baby from the hospital but soon afterwards, I watched in disbelief as she gave my cot to Delina's mother, the one that I was saving for my little baby brother or sister!

It was all too much. I decided that this woman couldn't be trusted. She would have to be watched.

So, when Delina, her mother and her new baby brother, Riad, came to stay for a couple of days a few months later, I watched my mother like a hawk.

It wasn't long before I caught her betraying me again! I saw her through the glass pane in the kitchen door, taking what was mine again and giving it to her favourite!

That baby thief, Delina! First, she had taken my baby! Then, she had taken my cot. Next, she had taken my mother and NOW, she was after my Ribena!

Well, I wasn't having it! This was the last straw. I was going to teach her a lesson! She was never going to steal from me again. NEVER! I'd show her!

So, I tore down the hallway towards the kitchen sounding a shrill war cry, and bursting into the kitchen, I knocked the paper cup that held the Ribena out of Delina's hand and onto the kitchen floor!

A splodge of deep purple liquid began forming on the tiled floor with rivulets branching out here and there, and over this splodge, stood I with my little hands on my hips and determination on my face to scare the thief, screaming for all that I was worth.

My mother knew she was beaten at this point.

"I'm sorry," she said sheepishly to Delina's mother. *"I don't think it will be possible for you to stay at this time after all. She doesn't seem to be settling very well. I'm really sorry."*

"I understand," replied Delina's mother with a forgiving smile and pretty soon after that, they left, all three of them, Delina, her mum and their "stolen" baby.

They had come to stay for three nights. Thanks to my outrage, they left the same day.

Chapter Five– "Tell Him I'm Dead!"

Over time, I learned to forgive Delina for stealing my baby. Actually, it was never really my baby. Delina's mother had been joking when she said I could have it!

She had been pregnant at the time so it was HER baby really but I didn't know that at the time. I believed her when she told me that there was a baby on the way for me. I didn't know she was joking. How could I? I was only three.

My mum and Delina's mum were friends and so, my mum would often take me to Delina's house to play with her and the baby while she and Delina's mum sat in the kitchen and talked about whatever grown-ups talked about.

You would think that after our childish competition about whose Mummy would get them a baby first, Delina would be grateful to have a baby brother!

You'd think she'd be especially nice to him after the tug of war we'd had over him just four years earlier.

Not so.

If there was one thing that girl loved to do, it was teasing her baby brother!

"Tell him I'm dead!" she'd whisper when I would go over and then, she'd lie really still on the floor as I'd groan to myself and think, "Oh no, not again!"

Delina was two years older than me so I felt I had to do whatever she told me to do because she was older so I'd sigh to myself and say to her baby brother,

"Riad, Delina's dead."

He'd look up at me with a frown and then he'd shake his head and say, *"No, she's not. She's not dead!"*

Then, he'd toddle over to where his naughty big sister was lying perfectly still on the floor and he'd tickle her.

I have no idea how Delina kept a straight face but she did!

When he'd get no response, he'd stick his finger up her nose and wiggle it and then, wiggle it some more.

Still, no response.

Then, he'd sit on her!

Still, no response although, if you looked really closely, you might see the beginnings of a smile, a tiny hint of one if you looked closely enough.

Then, finally when he'd had enough, he'd run down to the kitchen to his mum and announce in a mournful voice,

"Mummy, Denna's died again!"

Delina's mother would roll her eyes and say,

"All right. Never mind. You go upstairs and play."

She knew what her older child was like. She had done this so many times before.

Stressing out her baby brother, pretending she was dead, wasn't all she did to him!

When her mother wasn't around, she would do even worse and what's more, she always had to get me involved like the time she taught us silly songs about farts and made me sing them and made her brother act as if he was farting!

Delina taught us a song about Batman and Robin and it went like this....

"Batman and Robin

Going up the highway

Robin done a f..rt

He paralysed the wheel

The wheel couldn't take it

The car fell apart

All because of Robin

And his supersonic f..rt!"

And guess who she chose to do supersonic f..rts like Robin? Yes, you've guessed it, her poor little baby brother!

Just as I used to look up to Delina because she was two years older, Riad used to look up to us both because he was only four and we were eight and ten. So, he used to do whatever we told him to do. He thought we were grown-ups!

We used to hold hands and dance around him as we sang about Batman and Robin and Robin's supersonic f..rts and whenever we said the f.... word, Riad had to stick out his little bottom and blow a massive raspberry with his mouth!

Sometimes, their mother used to come upstairs and check on us. She'd ask us if we were all right and Delina would look up at her mum with her big, wide innocent eyes and her mother would smile and pat us on the head and tell us that we were good girls for looking after her baby brother.

Then, she'd go back down to the kitchen again to chat with my mother.

I have to admit I felt bad sometimes. She was only proud of us because she thought we were nice little girls, taking good care of Delina's baby brother.

She didn't know we were making him do supersonic farts.

Chapter Six- Settled For A Ladybird!

By the time I was five, I had realised that I was always going to be an only child whether I liked it or not. There was never going to be a baby brother or sister for me.

So I learned to negotiate. By the time I was four, I had lowered my sights and I had asked my mother for a cat. I didn't get one of those either so in the end, in desperation, I settled for a ladybird!

I think I was what they call "deprived."

I found Matilda on a leaf in a hedge outside our building. She was just minding her own business when I scooped her up and put her gently in a matchbox and later, transferred her to a flowerpot full of soil with a plant in it in our living room.

I realised that a ladybird was all I was going to get in life so I had to make do with Matilda. All was going well or so it seemed for a couple of days until the day when I sprayed her with perfume and she suddenly stopped moving. I was devastated. I couldn't understand it. Mum loved perfume. I loved it. Why did Matilda stop moving when I sprayed her all over with perfume? I was just being kind.

When Mum had taken me to the local Infants School in January 1977 to start school, I talked the headmistress Mrs White's ears off, talking excitedly about ladybirds, caterpillars and butterflies and I even invited her back to ours to come and meet my ladybird!

The headmistress was supposed to interview me but the poor woman couldn't get a word in edgeways! I thought we were best friends because she had the same wallpaper as us! Mum said I kept bobbing up and down in my seat, excitedly saying,

"Look Mummy! Look! She's got the same wallpaper as us! She's got the same wallpaper as us!"

I talked so much that in the end, my mother snapped and said crossly,

"Danita, STOP talking! Don't drive the lady mad!"

So, I stopped.

Mrs White must have liked me though because she gave me a place at her school.

Maybe, I was a chatterbox at school because I was a lonely, only child at home. It's no fun being the only child among two adults. I had to live in my imagination most of the time.

Grown-ups can be so different to kids. They feel like a different species sometimes.

They don't like to move much. They mostly like to sit around and talk. They don't play hopscotch. They don't run around playing Kiss Chase or Tag in their break, like kids do in the school playground in their breaks.

They don't do handstands or stand on their heads. They don't jump up and down on their parents' beds. They don't like to MOVE like kids do.

Most grown-ups don't try to fly like children do. My parents would never join me in jumping off the sofa, flapping my arms, expecting to take off and fly! No grown up would try to fly using Mum's kitchen broom like I did because that's how Meg flew in the book we were reading at school called Meg and Mog! I thought that if Meg could do it, I could do it too, so I tried and tried and tried but I never did manage to fly!

Then, there were the times I used to stand by the window singing *"Rain, Rain, go away,"* and when the rain used to stop, I used to think the whole of England should be thanking me because I had made the rain go away!

I used to spin round and round in my living room singing *"Wonder woman! Wonder woman!"* and actually expected to turn into Wonder Woman!

What grown up is going to do that with a kid? Grown-ups just like to sit around talking or reading or watching TV so, it can be boring for a kid to be stuck with a couple of "giants" all the time. This was why I hated being an only child. School was the only time I got to be with other kids, with other people who had as much energy as me.

At home, I read books, played with dolls and watched TV. At school, I sped around the playground with other children at playtimes but at home, life wasn't so exciting. I had to live in my imagination most of the time.

Mum wouldn't get me a real baby but she bought me lots of dolls to play with. My babies were made of plastic and they were born in a factory.

First, there were my twins, Johnny and Julie. They were my first-born and they were really shy.

Then, there was Marie. She was mother's little helper. She was my favourite, always helping me in the kitchen and with the housework. She was my good girl and her teachers' pet. She never let me down.

Then, there were my two youngest, Molly and Shirley. They were always up to mischief, getting into scrapes and getting caught with chocolate on their face or with their hands in the biscuit tin!

Being an only child, I lived in the world of my imagination when I was at home. That's when I wasn't staring out of the window gazing longingly at the kids from the neighbourhood playing outside with each other. They seemed as if they were having so much fun. I longed to join them.

There was a time, they used to call for me to go outside and play with them and I'd beg my mother to let me outside and play but the answer was always *"no,"* so I'd have to say,

"Sorry, I can't come out to play. My mummy says I can't. Sorry. I'm really sorry."

They stopped calling for me after a while because the answer was always the same.

So, I used to watch them longingly from the window, wishing I could join in and play with them while stuck at home playing with my dollies, reading fairy stories and living in the world of my imagination, a lonely only...

GROWN UPS WHO'VE DONE THINGS WITH THEIR BITS (TO MAKE BABIES).

My mum did it ONCE in 1970 because she was DESPERATE to have me and after that, she NEVER did it again. That's why I'm an only child because MY mum's not like that!

Mr and Mrs Thatcher did it ONCE in 1952. Luckily for them, they had two babies in one go so they NEVER had to do it again!

The Queen and Prince Philip

Four babies = four times.

Four times.

FOUR TIMES!!!

Am I "deprived?"

Asked for a baby

Asked for a cat

Settled for a ladybird!

Chapter Seven- Mr Giles and The Verbal Table Tests

They say you never forget a good teacher and Mr Giles was one of those so even though I left my first school back in Stockwell three years ago in 1979, I have never forgotten him!

Mr Giles was tall and slim with brown hair, a brown beard and twinkly, smiley brown eyes. He was a teacher who loved his job and us. Thanks to all the things he did for us, he should have won a teaching award!

"What made him so special?" you might ask. Well, it could be his cheerful personality or it could be because of all the things he did to make us learn.

On cold, gloomy, drizzly days when we couldn't run around in the playground or days when the skies were pouring down with rain, he'd gather us in the hall at break-times and make us go up onto the podium and tell jokes! It was his way of getting us to be brave and to talk in front of lots of people.

When our teachers were ill or away, he used to come in and teach us himself! One time when we were doing PE and running around in the hall in our bare feet, I somehow got under his feet and because he was so tall and I was so small, he didn't see me when he trod heavily on my toe!

Hearing a high-pitched scream, Mr Giles looked down to see a seven- year-old sobbing hysterically, holding her toe! I still remember when he picked me up to comfort me, thinking to myself,

"I'm on an aeroplane!" as I could see the tops of my friends' heads for the first time while cradled in my teacher's arms.

It wasn't just his caring personality that made him special. It was all the thoughtful things he did to make us want to learn that made him such a great teacher, things like Scholar of the Week. Every week, Mr Giles would ask all the class teachers which child had worked the hardest and done the best work. Every one of the teachers would name the child in their class who had worked the hardest as "Scholar of the Week."

Mr Giles would call out the names of the Scholars of the Week at the end of assembly, and he'd take a polaroid picture of us together, some of us kneeling, some of us standing, all of us, smiling and he'd pin that photo on the noticeboard outside his office for a week under a huge sign that read Scholars of the Week! He'd make sure that we were appreciated for working hard. He made us feel that it paid to be well behaved.

That wasn't all he did though. He started to do something to make us want to learn our times tables because really, who wants to learn times tables? Yet, the amazing Mr Giles found a way to make sure that we did!

If you learned your two times tables, he'd give you a packet of crayons. For the 3 times tables to the 12 times tables, you could get a felt tip pen of any colour in assembly the next day. He'd call you up to the podium and there in a box, there would be a rainbow of felt tip pens of all different colours and you could pick a different colour after each times table test you passed!

When you're seven, felt tip pens are a status symbol. If you have felt tip pens, it means that you have arrived. You are someone. You're not just a little kid any more scribbling with crayons. You're a big kid. You have PENS. You're being trusted with PENS like a grown-up!

I'll never forget the day I came home and said to my mum,

"Mummy, guess what? Elissa did her two times tables and she won a prize! Mr Giles gave her a packet of crayons!"

My mother's eyes were wide like saucers as she replied,

"Elissa did her two times tables? Why didn't YOU do your two times tables?

And that's how it began. After that, my mother was unstoppable. She bought me one of those red, Silvine notebooks you can get at the newsagents, you know the ones with all the times tables on the back of them, and she decided that I was going to learn all the times tables and win every prize that was going!

She made me learn my two times tables, my three times tables, my four times tables, my five times tables all the way up to my twelve times tables! Mr Giles got used to me, tugging at his sleeve every week, saying, *"Mr Giles, can I tell you my times tables please?" There* was never a bad time for this teacher. He always had time for us.

"Hmmm.. Whose class are you in? What is your name?" he'd ask as he pulled out a notebook from his breast pocket before letting me recite a different times table every week!

The next day, he'd announce in assembly,

"Danita Khan from Mrs Smith's class did her 7 times tables yesterday. Come up and get your prize Danita,"

and so, I would walk up onto that stage and get a new colour felt tip pen every week. I had every colour of the rainbow by the time I got to my twelve times tables! I was officially a big girl now who owned a lot of pens! I was not just some baby, scribbling with crayons or writing with pencils! I was someone. I had PENS!

You might think that passing all the times tables up to 12 at the age of seven would be enough for anyone but that was not enough for my mother, not after she heard about the verbal table test!

The verbal table test was a verbal test that you took on stage in front of the entire junior school in assembly. Mr Giles fired ten questions from any of the 12 times tables at you and you had to answer correctly within three seconds! None of the eleven-year-olds had done it so my pushy, teacher mother decided that I was going to do it at the age of seven!

She went over all the times tables with me again and again for weeks so that I could not fail.

Finally, the big day arrived and to say I was terrified would be an understatement! My heart was pounding and my knees felt as if they were made of jelly as I made my way up on to the podium to stand beside Mr Giles.

Looking out onto the sea of expectant faces made my nerves even worse.

"Thanks Mummy," I thought to myself, *"Thanks a lot!"*

Before I could run, Mr Giles beamed at me before asking,

"So Danita, are you ready? Are you feeling brave?"

I found myself nodding even though I was feeling anything but brave. I was afraid that any minute, I might bring my breakfast back up!

With a strained smile, I looked up, up and up into the kind face of the smiling teacher who loomed over me like a skyscraper.

"Ready?" he asked again.

I knew I never would be but still, I whispered a very nervous, *"yes."*

"OK then, everyone wish her luck and here we go! Can you tell me Danita what do I get if I multiply 7 five times, what's 5 times 7?"

And that was when it happened.

No one could have known what I would do next. Even, I didn't know! Maybe because of my nerves, maybe because of over-excitement, when the words left his mouth, I did something

I hadn't planned to do, something embarrassing!

My feet sprang off the podium as I leapt excitedly up into the air, shouting, "THIRTY FIVE!" before landing back on my feet again!

Well, Mr Giles wasn't expecting that and neither was the rest of the school! The whole of the junior school had just seen me do the leap and shriek and everyone fell about laughing!

I must have looked so funny, this little seven-year-old girl with pigtails leaping up into the air and screeching every time Mr Giles asked me a question. I did it again and again every time he asked me a question. I couldn't help myself. It was my nerves!

And it was my nerves that got the better of me so in the end, when he asked me,

"What's eight times nine?" I was flummoxed. I failed.

Still, it wasn't that bad. I had managed to entertain the entire junior school in assembly that morning. I had given everyone a good laugh!

"Never mind Danita. Better luck next time," Mr Giles consoled me as I made my way off the podium, feeling a bit wobbly, and headed back to where my classmates were sitting, after having made a fool of myself!

I knew there was going to be a next time because when I got home and told my mum what had happened, she said briskly,

"Well, if at first, you don't succeed, try, try again!"

I knew then that there was no way out of it.

I was going to have to do it again!

It was a couple of weeks before Mum started coaching me again, going over the times tables again on the back of that red Silvine exercise book!

I was not very enthusiastic to say the least because I wasn't keen on times tables after the last time, and unlike the last time, this time, my mother got stressed. I heard her saying to Delina's mum on the phone,

"I don't know what to do with this child. She's just not motivated. She doesn't take life seriously."

I was SEVEN at the time.

"You'll fail again if you don't try harder," she'd warn me, *"You'll fail again!"*

"If at first, you don't succeed, try, try again. You don't give up. You try again. If you fall, you get up again and again and again!"

That was my mother's motto.

My mother would not give up. She was determined. She went on and on and on at me to try, try again!

So, I had no choice. I had to try again!

The next time I got up onto that podium with Mr Giles, to everyone's astonishment, I didn't leap again! This time, I stood my ground.

When he asked me, *"What's 8 x 7?"* and I replied *"Fifty six!",* my feet stayed firmly on the ground even though I jerked a little, trying to stop myself from jumping up in excitement like I did the last time!

Mr Giles looked at the kids sitting on the floor of the hall. He grinned and said,

"She's calmed down this time!"

And everyone laughed, remembering how funny I had been the last time that I had tried to do the verbal times table test!

All I can say is that calming down must have helped me because this time, when Mr Giles asked me what 8 x 9 was, I remembered that it was 72.

I passed.

My classmates were beaming as I made my way back to them this time. One of them even said to me, *"We're proud of you. You're one of us and you beat the fourth years."* It was a lovely feeling.

My mum had been right when she had said to me, *"If at first, you don't succeed, try, try again!"* She had made me face my fears and try again and this time, I had succeeded. No one was laughing any more. People were proud of me.

Not only were my friends proud of me but Mrs Harding from no. 31 who lived down the road, knitted jumpers for me and said she was my English granny, bought me a couple of beautiful, glossy, hard-backed encyclopaedias!

I found them on my doorstep one morning when I was heading off for school and when I went over to number 31 to thank her after school, she gave me a hug and she said, *"I heard you were a bit of a brain."* Another neighbour, Pat whose twins were at school with me, beamed at me and said, *"Aren't you a clever little girl?"*

Mum was right. *"If at first you don't succeed, try, try again."*

Having said that, I do think that all the praise went to my mum's head a little. She started suspecting that her child might be a bit of a genius and she got carried away!

After I became the first child in the school to pass the verbal table test, she took me to Madame Tussauds to learn about famous historical figures.

While we were there, she kept trying to get me to stand next to a skinny man in a funny outfit with little round glasses and I refused!

"Go on," she said smiling, *"Let me take a picture of you with the Mahatma. One day when you understand who he was, you will want to stand with him. Go on! Make mummy happy. Let me take a picture of you with Mr Gandhi."*

I looked at this skinny man in his funny outfit with little round spectacles on the end of his nose, and I was not impressed. This man had no fashion sense!

I thought to myself, *"Are you kidding? Have you seen what he is wearing?"* I refused to stand next to the skinny man in the funny outfit. I went and stood next to Mrs Thatcher instead!

My mother's hopes for me being a genius faded a little when she read what I had written about some of the world's leaders in Madame Tussauds in my note book after the visit.

She had asked me to do a summary of what I had learned on my visit to Madame Tussauds and guess what I had written in my little red

Silvine exercise book with the times tables on the back?

I had written:

Winston Churchill was a wealthy and a plump man and he died.

Lady Churchill lives in Kent.

Mr Gandhi had no fashion sense.

My mother decided to lay off me a bit after that and let me be a little kid instead of thinking that I was some great genius. She realised at this point that perhaps, she was expecting too much from her only child because, after all, in my defence, I was only seven at the time!

Chapter Eight- Miss Kay's Infant Class

In December 1979, my mother told me that there was no Santa Claus. I was eight at the time, and I refused to believe her. I thought she had got it wrong. I argued with my mother,

"No Mummy, there IS a Santa! I met him at nursery when I was four. Remember? Then, I met him again last year at school. He IS real!"

Mum looked unimpressed.

"No, that was just Mr Giles in a Santa suit," she replied calmly.

I was shocked. It never occurred to me that Mr Giles was Santa!

"I'm leaving your father and we're going abroad to be with family. I need money to send you to a good school out there. There's no money for Christmas presents this year. I need you to be a big girl. I need you to understand that."

And that was that, the end of my childhood. No more Santa. No more Rudolph, the red nosed reindeer leading the sleigh and elves making presents for kids in the North Pole!

That's the day I finally understood why back in 1977, Santa had bought the normal sized Lego for my friends, Hannah and Jimmy, and giant Lego for me!

When I was six, my friends Jimmy, Hannah and I had all written letters to Santa, asking for Lego. We all got the Lego but what was strange was how Jimmy and Hannah got the normal sized Lego whereas for some unknown reason, Santa had given me the giant Lego for babies even though we were all the same age!

I complained to my mother about being given the baby Lego with the giant bricks and asked why Santa would treat me differently from my friends.

Mum replied, *"Ah well, you see, Shanta told me he was worried about you that if you got the small Lego pieces, you could accidentally swallow a piece, choke and die! So, he got you the big Lego pieces so that you don't swallow, choke and die."*

I was starting to think at this point that Santa was a bit weird.

"But...how come he didn't do that to Hannah or Jimmy? They're six like me. How come he gave THEM the normal sized Lego? How come he didn't worry that they would swallow, choke and die? How come he treated ME like a baby?"

My mother looked a bit shifty as she answered,

"We...ell, sometimes, he forgets because he has so many children to deliver presents for. Now, eat your dinner!"

1977 had been a good year. It was the year I started school in January after the interview with Mrs White about the butterflies, caterpillars and ladybirds! I was put in Miss Kay's class where I found a friend who I had known at nursery. Hannah and I had been at a nursery run by Italian nuns where we used to breathe in the comforting aroma of Italian pasta soup every day and race tortoises in the back yard!

It was good to see a familiar face but it wasn't long before I made new friends as well like Jimmy.

1977 was the year of the Silver Jubilee. It had been twenty five years since Queen Elizabeth II had taken the throne and there were parties held in streets all across London. The streets were lined with children waving flags they had made in school to greet the queen. Miss Kay taught us how to make them and then, on the big day, we were taken out by the teachers to stand by the road and wave the flags we had made over the week!

As we stood by the roadside chanting, *"We want the queen! We want the queen!"* the children standing on the opposite side of the road from a neighbouring primary school started chanting it as well!

Then, our lot started pulling faces, sticking out tongues and yelling,

"Copycat! Copycat!

"Nerh...nerh nerh...nerh nerh!"

And then, after what felt like ages waiting for the queen and Prince Philip to arrive, they sped by in a flash and we hardly got a good look at them! They went by so fast that people were left arguing about what colour she was wearing!

Speaking of colour, being a Londoner, my friends were all the colours of the rainbow. Well, maybe not all the colours of a rainbow. I didn't have any red or orange or green friends or violent or indigo! I mean all the colours that humans came in!

My best friend, Hannah was Irish. She was a kind of pinky, peach colour and my other best friend, Jimmy, had parents from the Caribbean, so he had black hair and brown skin.

Hannah used to come to my house a lot because she lived nearby and back then, I thought her granny was the best granny in the world because she always had sweets! She had chocolate buttons sprinkled with hundreds and thousands and because I was Hannah's friend from nursery and now, infants as well, she always gave me some.

But however nice Hannah's nanny was, Hannah was a lonely only like me so one day, we hatched a plan to be together forever like sisters!

Hannah had come to my house to play, dropped off by her nan and when it was time for her to go home, we decided that she was going to stay with me forever so that we could be sisters!

So, I hid her under the bedcovers in my bed and when my parents came to walk her home to her nan's, I said,

"Hannah's not here. She's gone home."

My parents were not convinced. They loomed over my bed looking serious, and pointing to the child-shaped lump next to me under the covers, my mother said,

"No, she has NOT gone home and you know she has to go home to her nanny otherwise her nanny will worry."

At this point, I burst into tears as my mother pulled back the covers to reveal Hannah curled up in a little ball! My plan to have a sister had failed yet again, just as my plan to get a baby brother or sister two years earlier had failed.

Once again, I had to face the fact that I was doomed to be an only child!

At school, there was my other best friend, my friend, Jimmy.

I'll never forget the time he said to Miss Kay,

"Miss, I won't be here on Thursday because I'm going to be ill!"

Or the time that Hannah got into trouble with Miss Kay for asking an unspeakable question!

We had been sitting on the mat on the floor while Miss Kay sat on a chair facing us as she read us a story. She usually read us Ladybird books about Peter and Jane and Pat, the dog.

Peter was a little boy who was always helping Daddy in the garden while Jane helped Mummy in the kitchen and around the house!

Well, one day, Miss Kay was reading us one of the Ladybird stories at story time and I noticed Hannah behaving in a strange way. It looked as if Hannah was trying to look up Miss Kay's skirt! She kept trying and trying until finally, she put up her hand.

"Yes, Hannah?" asked Miss Kay expectantly, expecting a question about the story.

That's when Hannah dropped a clanger when she asked innocently,

"Miss, what colour knickers have you got on?"

Miss Kay did not look amused. There was a sharp intake of breath before she said sternly,

"Hannah, come here please. Give me your hand."

Hannah put out her hand and Miss Kay gave her a light tap on her palm with a ruler before saying sternly,

"Go and stand in the corner!"

Poor Hannah looked confused. There was a look on her face that was saying,*"What have I done?"*

She seemed genuinely curious about the colour of Miss Kay's knickers and she didn't know why she couldn't just ask and find out!

How could Hannah that know that asking Miss Kay about the colour of her knickers was any different to asking her about the colour of her socks? She was only six at the time.

The world of the grown-ups can be quite confusing for a six-year-old. You're never quite sure what you're allowed to say and what you're not allowed to say or when they might get cross.

So, as Miss Kay continued to read to her class of six-year-olds, poor little Hannah stood facing the wall in the corner and kept looking back over her shoulder wistfully at the rest of us, sitting there comfortably on the mat.

Chapter Nine- Jimmy, Hannah, Mavis and Me!

My friend Jimmy and I used to play Cowboys and Indians in the playground back in 1977 but at six years old, we could be a bit confused sometimes. When we played Cowboys and Indians, I used to be a cowboy and Jimmy used to be a horse! It never occurred to me to be an Indian and I'll never know why Jimmy wanted to be a horse!

I'd sit on his back in the playground and say, *"Gee up horsey!"* and he'd reply with a hearty *"NEIGH!"*

I could never imagine Miss Kay jumping onto Mr Giles's back and saying, *"Gee up horsey!"* but when you're six, this is considered normal!

Then again, what IS normal? I just found out how grown ups make babies and that doesn't seem very normal to me, but grown-ups think it's normal!

Apart from playing Cowboys and Indians, there were times when we all used to compete with each other saying,

"Look! Look at me! I got muscles!"

We'd all roll up our sleeves, get out our skinny, six year old arms and compare our non-existent "muscles!"

Being the only Indian girl in my class, I had special status and there were times when my friends used to dance around me in a circle in the playground singing, *"Brown girl in the ring, tra la lalala! There's a brown girl in the ring, tra la lalalala!"* while I stood there looking all smug in the centre, enjoying being the centre of attention, one of the few brown girls in the class and the only brown girl in the ring!

This was the nineteen seventies, the decade of weird fashion, a time when grown-ups wore giant, chunky platform boots and flared trousers and most of us kids had jumpsuits with flared trousers and a patch at the top with a picture of celebrities on them!

I had a blue onesie with a picture of Starsky and Hutch on it, two handsome police officers in a TV show, and Hannah had a pink one with Abba on hers.

Then, there was the Fonz from Happy Days, another American TV show. He was an Italian American man who had his hair slicked back and who wore a leather jacket, and he used to go around, giving people the thumbs up and talking about being "cool." We used to stick our thumbs up like Fonzie in the show and say in an American accent, *"The Fonz is cool!"*

That's when we weren't running around the playground in slow motion, pretending to be superheroes like the Bionic Woman or the Six Million Dollar Man!

The best thing about our class though was our class pet. While I'd had to settle for a lady bird at home, at school, we had a real, live guinea pig! Her name was Mavis and she was the sweetest little class pet ever! All the children loved her and in the school holidays, there was always some lucky kid who got to take her home.

Mavis was a gorgeous little guinea pig with black and white fur, a cute little pink nose and bright, shining eyes. And she loved to squeak! She was one very talkative little piggie!

When Miss Kay and another teacher used to take us out for walks, we used to collect dandelions for Mavis because she loved them.

On school outings, we used to be put into pairs and we'd walk holding the hand of our partner. There would be a teacher at the front of the line of kids to lead us as we moved forward two by two with a teacher at the back, watching over us all.

Hannah was normally my partner and whenever we were taken out, we'd try and look for dandelions for Mavis! As soon as we got back to school, we'd head for her cage which always smelled of sawdust and we'd shove the flowers into her cage.

"Eeek!" she'd squeak. *"Eek! Eek! Eek*!" and she'd bound up excitedly to us, her black eyes shining like diamonds in her smiley little face as we shoved as many dandelions as we could into her sawdusty home.

Much as I loved ladybirds, there was no comparison between Mavis and Matilda. Mavis was my first real pet even though I had to share her with twenty four other kids, and even at the age of six, I knew that she would live in my heart forever.

Aged three in 1974-5. This was when I used to beg my mother for a baby brother or sister. I never got one though!

Miss Kay's class of six-year-olds, 1977.

Aged five in 1976-7. This was around the time when I started school after interviewing the

headmistress, Mrs White, about ladybirds, caterpillars and butterflies!

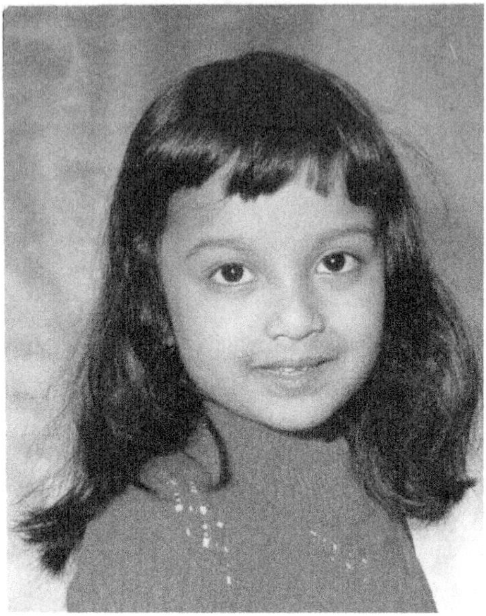

Chapter Ten- Single Parent Family

In December 1979, after my parents split up, my mother took me to Asia to live as part of an extended family. There were seven of us in one big apartment, my mum, her two sisters, me and my baby cousin and a live-in lady who cooked and cleaned. Plus, there was another lady who used to come in daily to wash our clothes.

These women did the housework while my mother and her sisters went to work. My mum and her sister worked at the British Embassy and their younger sister worked in a bank.

The lady who lived in with us was a bit like a nanny to me as well but in India and in Bangladesh, nannies are called ayahs.

Unlike my mother who wasn't big on physical displays of affection, Boo was!

Sometimes, she'd sit me on her lap and tell me stories in Bengali about ghosts and ghouls and the devil and on the rare occasions when my own mother used to try and smack me, Boo would stand boldly between us and shield me with her body.

"No, she hasn't done anything. She's been a good girl. She's always a good girl," she'd say in Bengali to my mother and every time my mother would try and get round Boo, Boo would turn around so that I was hidden behind her.

It was like having a second mother.

Most schools in the country back in 1980 taught students in Bengali so Mum had to pay for me to go to an international English medium school where all the children of the embassy workers and ex pats went. The school was run by nuns called Sister Theresa and Sister Barbara. It had huge green playing fields, and the teachers were really strict. We had Indian dance lessons. We had tiffin at ten and exams every month because the standards were so high. We were doing mixed integers in maths and the children's versions of classics like Oliver Twist and David Copperfield at the age of ten!

Mum paid for the school from the sale of the London flat that my parents sold when they separated, and when the money ran out after paying for this expensive school, we had to come back to London, and coming back was hard.

For two whole years, I had lived in a big apartment with many rooms filled with many people and suddenly, we were back in England, just the two of us, renting a bedroom in someone's family home. I missed our extended family and all the fun we had in the evenings when we'd all get together and chat.

For the first time, I felt what it was to be a single parent family. My mother and I were on our own and it felt like it!

Mum contacted Gingerbread, a charity that supported single parent families and she applied for a council house. Back in the seventies, we had lived in our own flat in Stockwell but because of my parents separating, selling the flat and splitting the money from the sale, we had become homeless.

My mother had been happy in her own country, surrounded by her family and friends but she had come back for me so that I would have English as my first language and coming back led to something called depression.

Because she couldn't get cheap childcare in London like she could abroad (Boo used to look after me when she was at work) and because of her depression, Mum couldn't work and money was tight.

I realised how bad things were one day when we had gone out shopping and while engrossed in reading a magazine in a shop, I had absent-mindedly left a bag of shopping behind!

I was walking happily homewards with my mother when suddenly, she noticed that something was missing.

"Danita, where is the shopping?"

Imagine my horror when I realised that I had left the shopping behind somewhere. I didn't know where.

"WHERE is the shopping?" she repeated slowly and deliberately as if she was trying to control emotions that were running high like a river that was about to burst its banks.

"I- I don't know," I admitted, terrified, shaking inside because I had a feeling that a storm was about to erupt.

"WHAT do you mean you don't know? What do you mean you don't know?" she repeated her voice rising sharply.

"I'm...I'm sorry Mum. I- I can't remember. I don't know. I think I must have left it somewhere by... by mistake."

"What do you mean you've left it. You've left it where? WHERE? There was £20 worth of shopping in that bag! What are we going to eat for the rest of the week? Do you think that money grows on trees? Do you think I am made of money? Do you think that I'm a millionaire? "

"No Mum. No."

"It's not as if your father pays a penny! I have to do it all. What do you think we are going to eat now, now that you've lost half the shopping, day-dreaming? You SILLY GIRL!"

My mother's eyes were blazing. I had never seen her so angry before. It felt as if she hated me and to my horror, she kept on screaming at me right there in the middle of the road in front of strangers, lots of strangers. I wanted to die. It was so embarrassing. People were staring.

I'd never seen my mother lose it like that. It was frightening. I wanted to run. I wanted to get away, far, far away from it all, parents fighting, parents divorcing, mothers getting depressed, and screaming hysterically at their kids in the street because they couldn't cope!

She was screaming at me. She was getting hysterical in the street, in front of everyone! People were staring at her. People were staring at me and so I did the only thing I felt I could do. I ran.

I ran as fast as I could to get away from my mother. I ran and I ran and I ran, and I would have kept on running if a lady with a kind face hadn't stopped me.

She had seen what had happened. I think she felt sorry for me. She looked about my mother's age. She was an African/Caribbean lady.

She saw the terror in my eyes and she knew I needed someone to be kind. She came up to me, pity in her eyes and she spoke to me gently, soothing me by being gentle, by being kind.

"Don't worry darling. Go on back to your mother. Go on. Everything will be all right. You'll see. It will be all right. Don't worry. Go on back to Mum. Go on darling. Be brave. Everything's gonna be fine."

It didn't feel as if things were going to be fine. It didn't feel as if things were ever going to be all right but I knew I had to go back. I had to face the music. I had to face my mum. Where else was I going to go? There was nowhere I could go.

I decided to re-trace my steps and go back to all the shops we had been to with the hope that maybe the bag was still there. Then again, this was London. I didn't hold out much hope.

I made a note to myself that day NEVER to lose a shopping bag again!

Chapter Eleven- Chalkhill

After coming back from spending time with family abroad, we lived in a rented room in the house of a family of strangers in North London. We only had a bedroom to ourselves and we had to share the bathroom and the kitchen with the strangers who were the owners of the house. We lived like that for almost a year.

Then, finally, in October 1982, my mother told me that we were moving to a council flat on Chalkhill Estate. Chalkhill Estate was a large white council estate with lots of buildings that had lots of flats with long walkways. We had been there a few times before to visit a family we knew so I knew it well.

A week before we moved in, disaster struck. A young Asian woman of twenty-five was murdered on the estate! The reporter in the paper said that she was murdered on Redcliffe Walk and guess where we were moving to? You've guessed it! Redcliffe Walk!

My mother went into overdrive. She was hysterical! I heard her complaining to Delina's mum on the phone.

"I never thought I'd be reduced to raising MY child in one of those places! I have to move to this dangerous place with my little girl. What is going to happen to us?"

Unlike parents who love each other and are happy together who buy a home and then, work to buy an even better home, my parents had hated each other and had been miserable together so they had split up and sold their home. They had each taken half of the money from the sale of the flat. My mum had spent her share on me, and he had spent his share on himself, and now, my mother and I were homeless.

So, now, here we were, moving to a notorious council estate where a young Asian girl had just been murdered!

On the day that we moved in, gangs of teenage boys of around sixteen or seventeen kept milling around, staring at us and our second-hand furniture.

The neighbour from next door, an English lady with a warm and friendly smile welcomed us to the neighbourhood but warned us,

"They're looking to see if you've got anything worth stealing."

They must have decided that we didn't have anything worth stealing because after that first day, they left us alone.

That didn't mean we had an easy time of it though because along with the nice people like the lady next door, there were some dodgy ones as well!

First there was Sharon, a skinny, scrawny girl who lived on the estate. She looked about my age, not more than eleven or twelve with long sandy hair and a skinny, scornful face and every time she saw us, she had to make a nasty comment about Asian people and curry!

Like many racist people, she thought that all brown people came from Pakistan. She seemed to think that the only country in Asia was Pakistan, and she was too lazy to say Pakistani so she used to say paki instead!

"Oi look! It's them two pakis again," she sneered one day as we were walking past her, minding our own business.

"You can always tell when there are pakis about! You can smell the curry a mile off."

I looked at my mother and my mother shook her head and told me to ignore her.

"Rise above it," she would always say. *"Don't go down to their level."*

But a few months later, something happened that was impossible to ignore.

My mother used to walk me back from school and one day as we were on the walkway, three teenage girls blocked our path as we were trying to get back to our flat.

The one who blocked our path was African/ Caribbean. The other two were white. She looked older than me. She looked about fifteen and as she loomed threateningly over me, she said to my mum,

"I'm going to throw your kid over the balcony 'cos I don't like pakis. They've taken over all the corner shops. Tell all the pakis to go home!"

My mother was horrified. She was shaking visibly as she replied,

"If you threaten my child again, I'll call the police. I will write to my MP! Don't threaten my child!"

The girl responded with*, "Just tell all the pakis to go home. All right?"*

Then, she looked at her mates for approval and they swaggered off, looking really pleased with themselves.

That was the first time my mother wrote to her MP, and it was the first of many letters she'd write to him over the two years and two months that we lived on that estate!

Chapter Twelve- God & Simon Le Bon

After we moved to the estate, my mother would never let me out of her sight. She would never let me out on my own! She said it was too dangerous. She hated having to live there.

I didn't like it much either but I didn't hate it as much as she did because a few of the children from my school lived on my estate and I used to watch them from my window, doing wheelies on their BMX bikes, wishing I could join them!

It was just like when I was a little girl, watching my friends in Stockwell, playing out together while I watched from the window because my anxious mother wouldn't let me out.

After school, I was bored. There's only so much TV you can watch. At eleven, I was still young enough to want to run around and do things. I wasn't a grown up yet!

To keep me busy, Mum used to take me to the library every week to borrow six books and read them at home and so, I became a bit of a bookworm.

Then, there was homework and housework and soap operas like Dallas and Dynasty where all the men and women were glamorous and looked like supermodels. I thought that everyone in America looked like Fallon and Jeff from Dynasty. I thought they were a nation of supermodels, the most beautiful people in the world.

On TV, there were sitcoms like Mork and Mindy. Mork was funny and Mindy was sweet. She had so much fun dealing with Mork and his alien ways like when he used to say,

"Nanu Nanu!" and sit on his head!

Of all the TV series though, my favourite, my absolute favourite, was The Kids from Fame!

The kids from Fame were all kids from broken homes like me. Older kids of seventeen with single parents, the Kids from Fame were talented teens with big dreams.

There was Bruno Martelli, the musical genius and protégé of Professor Shorofsky. Bruno was a modern-day Mozart with his adoring taxi-driver father who was so proud of his talented son, the musical prodigy. It was so sweet. You had to love Bruno and his dad. You wished so much that Bruno would make it.

Then, there was Doris, the singing sensation who lived in poverty with her single parent mother. How could you not love Doris? She was so bubbly and so hopeful with a head full of dreams.

And then, there was Coco Fernandez who had nothing but a dream of greatness and she WAS great! The way she flew through the air and defied gravity when she was dancing was awe-inspiring and amazing to see.

There were so many talented kids in the show and you wanted them so badly to make it because they all came from disadvantage. They had all suffered so much heartbreak so early on in life. They deserved to have some happiness after all that they had been through.

At the start of the show, someone leaps and does the splits in mid air and I was so inspired by this that I tried to do the same thing, only when I tried to do it, my slip-on shoe flew off my foot and ended up on another part of the road! I had to hop to my shoe to get it back. I looked really silly.

Apart from the Kids from Fame, there were the pop groups that kids my age followed obsessively. Most teenagers love music and lots of teenage girls fall in love with pop stars or film stars and dream of growing up and marrying them!

Back in December 1981 when my mother and I had just come back from being abroad, Delina showed me a picture of a man with a white stripe across his nose. She looked at me very, very seriously and she said solemnly,

"EVERYBODY loves this man Danita and you MUST love him too. Do you understand? Swear that you will always love him Dani. SWEAR!"

"Em..yeah, all right then," I said, a bit scared by her intensity. I was afraid that if I didn't love him, she might smack me!

I wasn't sure why I had to love this man with the white stripe across his nose but Delina was nearly thirteen and I was eleven and when you're eleven, if a thirteen-year-old tells you something, you feel you have to take them seriously.

Then, she told me that Duran Duran were the best band in the world and that I must love them too and I agreed with her on that one, although I loved Depeche Mode too especially their song, "See You," which was filmed in someone's local Woolworths! I loved the song with the video of the man taking photos in a photo booth with the smiling girl behind the counter while he was singing,

"All I wanna do is see you. Don't you know that it's true?"

I loved Depeche Mode but under Delina's influence, I began to love Duran Duran as well.

One time when the band went to Sri Lanka, Delina and I got together and wrote funny stories about them being chased by amorous locals in Sri Lanka, only we kept saying Sri Lankee by accident and Delina and I laughed so hard that she ran to the loo saying, *"I've got to wee! I've got to wee!"*

We used to love writing stories and she used to write funny stories where she and her friends Beverley and Maxine

stumbled across Duran Duran while walking down Oxford Street and in her story, Duran Duran's lead singer, Simon Le Bon, said to them,

"Oh my God! you're just the girls we've been looking for to be in our new video!"

And I used to think,

"Yeah right Delina, in your dreams! As if Simon Le Bon, the world-famous lead singer of Duran Duran is going to stop to talk to a load of thirteen-year-olds who are still at school. That's really gonna happen, NOT!"

But then, her influence did rub off onto me just as it did when we were little kids, and over time, I began to talk to Duran Duran's lead singer, Simon Le Bon myself!

When I say I used to talk to Simon Le Bon it wasn't exactly Simon Le Bon. It was actually a poster of Simon Le Bon! I'd put it up in a store-room that I had filled with cushions and made into a little den where I could hide away and day-dream.

When I got bored, cooped up in that flat, not being allowed to go out and ride a bike on the estate with the other kids, I used to hide away in the little den filled with cushions and posters that I had made out of a store-room, and I used to talk to Simon Le Bon about my problems. I felt like Simon understood. I felt like Simon cared.

Some days, I'd talk to God and some days, I'd talk to Simon Le Bon!

When I used to talk to them, neither of them ever talked back to me. It was just me, a lonely only child of eleven, stuck in a flat on a council estate talking AT them, hoping that they could hear me and hoping that they cared.

Chapter Thirteen- Leaving Primary

1982 has been quite a year. In March, I found out how babies are made. Then, a month later, at school, the teachers separated us from the boys to tell us about puberty. It was a talk about growing up and having periods. The boys had their own talk about puberty but I don't think it was about periods!

It was just as well they did the talk about periods and explained what to do because just after my eleventh birthday, I got mine!

I felt really embarrassed when I told my mum but she seemed fine but later, I heard her on the phone to Delina's mum and she was crying! She was crying because I had just had my first period at just eleven years old.

"My little girl's growing up so fast and I'm on my own. I don't know what to do. I don't know if I can keep her safe!"

Safe from what? Why would having your period make you less safe? Do people get bullied when they're on their period? Or was it dangerous to stop being a little girl and grow up to be a woman and if so, why? Why was she crying? Had I done something wrong by not staying her little girl, by growing up and having my period at eleven?

I didn't feel like a woman even with my period! I was still running around, playing Tag in the playground with my friends, colouring in my colouring-in books, and playing with my Tiny Tears doll, Courtney. I wasn't even a teenager yet and I had a feeling that I wouldn't feel like a grown up for a very long time. So, why was my mother crying?

She cheered up a bit a few weeks later when we found out I'd got a place at a good secondary school.

Miss Ellis told my mum she was a bit worried about me though and she asked if I was OK because she said that she had seen me looking a bit "stricken" in recent months since the spring. (That was when I found out how babies are made). My mum reassured her that I was OK and that everything was fine at home.

Now that I'd got into one of the best schools, we needed to get the uniform. My mum took me to John Lewis to buy me a navy-blue blazer with the school insignia and some writing in Latin. I don't know what it means. No one speaks Latin in Chalkhill!

As well as the blazer, we bought two shirts, one light blue, one white, two navy skirts and a school tie.

After we'd got the school uniform, we went to a café for a bite to eat before going home where I could try on my new school uniform for big school!

As soon as we got home, and as soon as I put on the blazer, I could see it was too big. It was too loose on me and the arms were too long but Mum said that I'd grow into it. She said that she'd bought a bigger size on purpose because she couldn't afford to pay for a new blazer every year!

When I finally had it all on, the full uniform, I stood in front of my mother to show her how I looked in the uniform for big school and she got all emotional again! Her eyes were shining with tears as she looked at me and sighed,

"You look so grown up in that uniform. Where did the time go? How did you grow up so fast? One minute, I brought a little bundle home from the hospital and the next minute, she's growing up and going to secondary school! Pretty soon, you'll be all grown up. You won't be my little girl any more!"

I wasn't sure if my mother was happy or sad that I was going to be a grown up before long. She looked a bit wistful as if she longed for the old days when I was little and cute and needed her all the time and, at the same time, proud that I was growing up and would, one day, make my own way in the world.

To be honest, I'm not sure if I want to grow up and go out into the big, scary world out there.

Just five years ago when I was six, I lived in an exciting world full of amazing people like a smiley faced man called Santa who loved children and brought presents for us every year from the North Pole.

Then, there was a lovely, red-nosed reindeer called Rudolph who had triumphed over the bullies who'd been mean to him and who'd picked on him for his shiny, red nose!

Plus, there were superheroes who flew high up in the skies and put the villains bang to rights. There were fairies, an Easter bunny and a stork who brought babies from God!

Now, five years later, I live in a world where there are NO fairies, no superheroes flying around in cape and tights saving lives, no Wonder woman, no Easter bunny, no Santa, nothing!

Now, I live in a world of gangs and crime and council estates where single parent mothers don't feel safe. I live in a world of periods and period pain. I live in a world where grown-ups PEE in the street and do things with their bits!

When I was six, I was DESPERATE to grow up.

Now that I'm eleven, I'm not so sure...

Chapter Fourteen- Nineteen Eighty Four

The secondary school that Miss Ellis recommended really was as good as she said. With massive green playing fields, neat tennis courts and shiny, new language labs, my new school was one of the best equipped schools in the borough and the teachers were the best. Some of them were real characters!

In the first year, we had a geography teacher who used to throw our exercise books at us in class after he'd marked them. Books would come whizzing at us from across the room and we had to get into position to catch them. It was hard to tell whether we were in a geography lesson or a sports lesson sometimes!

Then, there's Mr Long, our English teacher. He's a real character as well. I think he's what they call, "eccentric." He gave us a strange assignment the other day. Out of the blue, he told us to write a story for homework called The Last Elephant.

I wrote a story about ivory hunters taking down an entire herd of elephants for their tusks but leaving a baby elephant alive because he's too young to have tusks.

I wrote about the mother elephant and the baby, fleeing for their lives and just when you think they're going to make it, the hunters get the mother. Her legs buckle under her and she crashes to the ground. The poor little baby elephant stands beside his dying mother and cries as she takes her last breath. He is the last elephant. Mr Long must have liked my story because he gave me an A for it!

In our second year at school, we got a new form teacher called Mr Whitehouse. He's our geography teacher as well, and unlike the last geography teacher, he doesn't launch our exercise books like missiles across the classroom after he's marked our homework!

I think he's quite cool really. The other day I called him Dad by accident. I nearly died of embarrassment! Luckily, he didn't seem to notice or if he did, he didn't show it. Thank God.

It's not just the teachers who are characters though. Some of the kids are really funny like Marsha who takes whoopee cushions into class and then, sits on them when the class is quiet and you can hear a pin drop.

She did that SIX times last week in a maths lesson until the teacher, Mr Alam couldn't take it anymore! At first, he ignored her. The kids in the class were all trying to keep a straight face, trying not to giggle as she did it again and again to try and get Mr Alam's attention. Well, it worked because after the sixth time she'd sat on that whoopee cushion, Mr Alam snapped and sent her with an order slip to F27 for disrupting the lesson!

F27 is where the naughty kids go when they're disrupting the class but Marsha wasn't going to go without a fight. She staged her own personal protest!

"But sir, it's not my fault! It's nature sir. It's nature. I have to express myself! I have to be free! Don't you want me to express myself? I need to be free!"

"Well, you can express yourself in F27. Marsha, take the order slip and go! You are disrupting my lesson!"

While Marsha and Mr Alam were arguing, the rest of us were trying to look as if we were concentrating on our work while trying not to laugh! School was never boring with so many colourful, eccentric, people about!

I was starting to love my new school.

Chapter Fifteen- Mean Girls

I wish I could say that everyone at high school was as likeable as the teachers and as loveable as Marsha, the class funny girl, but not everyone was as nice as them.

Secondary school isn't like primary school. There isn't the same cosy atmosphere of being in the same classroom with the same teacher most of the day and a few others coming into your classroom now and then.

Here, we have to move all day from classroom to classroom and we have lots of different teachers who specialise in different subjects and there are lots of big kids who are as big as the grown-ups!

In primary school when I did well, no-one minded. My friends nominated me to be one of the team captains in a quiz because they thought I could lead the team to victory. They didn't mind me doing well at primary school.

But in secondary school, I found out that there could be some girls who were mean.

If you did well, they hated you. They were nosy and didn't know how to mind their own business. They got obsessed with other people and how other people were doing and if you did well at school, they made it their business to give you a hard time!

There was this one girl, Karen, who asked me,

"Dani, are you pleased that you did well in the exams? Are you happy?"

I replied, *"Yes, I am. Thanks."* I was being honest. I thought she'd be happy for me.

She wasn't.

She started sneering at me and saying, *"She thinks she's so special because she did well. She's so pleased with herself. She's so full of herself!"*

I was shocked because I hadn't spoken to anyone my marks. How did she find out? Why would she know? My position in the form had been on my report card and I hadn't shown it to her so how did she know, and what was it to do with her? It was none of her business!

The next time when she asked me whether I was happy that I had done well, I just shrugged my shoulders and said,

"No. It's no big deal. I'm not bothered really."

I thought,

"I had better not say that I'm pleased because she'll get upset again!"

That day, I found out that no matter what I said, that girl would find something negative to say after sticking her nose in my business when she sneered and said,

"She's so big headed! Doing well is nothing to her. She thinks she's so special!"

I never said I was special because I never thought I was special or better than anyone else! The only reason I did well was because I WORKED TEN TIMES HARDER than anyone else!

While all the other kids were out with their friends having fun and being kids, I was stuck at home with an over-protective mother who wouldn't let me out!

Once I reached secondary school, my mother forced me to study indoors while other kids my age were being kids, having fun and going out with their friends!

She said I had to work hard for the bright future she wanted me to have! She said that education is the key to success. My mother is a teacher from a long line of teachers who believe that education is everything. My mother's father was a teacher and so was her grandfather Omar so my mother pushed and pushed and pushed me to work hard!

Also, unlike the kids who can afford to have a childhood and not study, I don't have a father to hand me everything on a plate like they do. I have to build a life for myself through honest, hard work. Why is this such a problem for these people?

I don't have a rich father to buy me a house. When I am older, if I want to get out of council housing, I have to get a good job to pay a mortgage. To get a good job, I need good grades. I need to WORK extra hard to get out of poverty because I am poor! My childhood is being sacrificed for these grades!

If they worked as hard as me, they would get good grades as well! I'm not better than them. I just work harder and keep my grades to myself. So, why are they so obsessed with me?

Why are they so obsessed with keeping poor single parents' kids down and stopping us from achieving when they have fathers to give them everything and we don't! It doesn't make sense.

Another girl, Lorraine stalked me the whole of play time in the playground one day, saying, *"Dani only got thirty-one! Dani only got thirty-one!"*

This was after she had been nosy and had stuck her nose in my business saying,

"Dani, what did you get in the test?"

I didn't tell her what I'd got on the test. She had asked me!

I had realised by now that some people didn't like to see other people be happy or to feel good about themselves so I tried to sound not very happy. I said apologetically,

"Erm.. I only got thirty-one."

This seemed to set her off so she spent the whole of play time following me and my friends, saying sarcastically,

"Dani only got thirty-one! Dani only got thirty-one!"

The test had been out of thirty-five marks and I found out later that she had scored fourteen marks in the test so she had got jealous when I had told her my mark at HER request after she had stuck her nose in my business and asked me!

What was I supposed to do? Brag? I was trying to be modest so that I didn't upset anyone when I said I got only thirty-one marks out of thirty-five. I mean I didn't do THAT well! It's not like I got full marks or anything!

What was really sad about it was that this girl has EVERYTHING I don't have but she has to resent the ONE good thing I have in my life.

She has TWO parents, a mum and a dad. Her dad works for the police and holds down a steady job unlike my father who ran away when child support was mentioned because he didn't want to pay for me!

My single parent mother is raising me in poverty on a council estate while she has a nice house and a police man for a father who is raising her and paying for her and not being mean to her mother!

My parents had split by the time I was eight because they hated each other but her parents love each other. She never saw her father hitting her mother when she was three like I did! She never had to go through that trauma.

Lorraine has a mother AND a father who love each other and are together! She has two older brothers who dote on her, the only girl, while I'm a lonely only who has to go through life alone without a sister or a brother! Unlike her, I never got brothers or sisters. I had to settle for a ladybird!

Yet, here she was getting jealous of me, the girl who has everything I have never had just because I had ONE good thing in my life, my grades! She couldn't even let me have that ONE good thing while she had everything I never had! She had to get jealous of someone who had less than her!

It should have been the other way around. I should have been jealous of her but I'm not jealous of her because I mind my own business and I don't mind other people being happy. Other people being miserable isn't going to make my life any better!

Even though I have nothing, no holidays, no nice things and I live on a rough council estate, I don't get jealous of anyone so why should anyone be jealous of me, especially people who have so much more than me?

All I'm trying to do is to work hard to build a better life and to get out of poverty because I don't have a dad to give me anything!

Why is that such a problem for these people?

Why do they have to be jealous of the kids of single parents who have less than them? It doesn't make sense!

People can be mean sometimes. Hopefully, when they get older, they wise up and get better. Can you imagine being that petty and jealous and mean when you're fifty?

How SAD would that be?

Chapter Sixteen- Boys & Other Problems

Now that we're in secondary school, people are starting to fall in love and go on dates. It's not like primary school. People are growing up.

My problem is that I'm not allowed to fall in love. I'm not allowed to date or to go out with a boy because I'm growing up between two cultures. It's hard enough being a teenager but growing up with a foot in two worlds makes it ten times harder.

There's a boy in my class called Steven. He's really cute. He's bigger than all the other boys. He towers above them. He seems too big for his seat sometimes. He's got a cute nose and fair hair and blue eyes but that's not why I like him. I like him because he's funny!

He likes to make a nuisance of himself with girls, teasing them and that includes me and my friends. For example, if a girl's name is Dana, he'll walk past her in the hall going,

"Dana dana dana dana dana dana dana dana BATMAN!"

I know it's not that funny but it's funny when he does it!

Then, there was the time when he found out that my best friend's mum calls her Pinky at home. She never heard the end of that one!

Thank God he never found out that my mother calls me Dinky at home! Can you imagine if he knew that we were Pinky and Dinky, me and my best friend?

We would have never heard the end of that one!

I make out that I'm really cross with him when he's being a pain but I like him really. I just can't show that I like him because of the culture that I come from. I'm not allowed to look at boys or date boys. It's so strict. You grow up. You get married and you marry in your faith because God has to come first. So, he's not of my faith and we're not old enough to get married so I can't even look at Steven and I can't ever tell him that I like him even though I do so I never go near him or at least, I never did until Mr Tugey came along!

Mr Tugey is this new and very cute Science teacher who looks about twenty-two years old. He's tall and slim with blue-grey eyes and brown hair. He's not much older than the sixth formers and with his boyish good looks, he is a target for the sixth form girls.

When we were first years, we'd stare in fascinated horror as some of the sixth form girls would sashay on up to him and flirt with him, a teacher!

"Hello Sir. How are YOU doing?" said one of the sixth form girls one day in a very breathy, flirty voice while batting her eyelashes at him and pouting.

"Look what that girl's doing to that teacher?" I squeaked as Mr Tugey turned bright red and turned away from the amorous school girl who was grinning all over her face, seeing how uncomfortable she had made him.

Mr Tugey looked so young that even some of the girls in our age group didn't take him seriously and would try and flirt with him even though they were only twelve years old!

So, one of the girls in my class would say,

"Sir, Kirsty fancies you!"

And Kirsty would reply,

"No sir. It's Selina who fancies you really!"

There was a lot of talk about people fancying the cute and young looking, new teacher who didn't look any older than the sixth formers and who didn't always seem to know what he was doing like the time he "punished" me for chatting to my friend, Paulami in class by making Steven, one of the cutest boys in my class, sit next to me!

I couldn't believe my luck!

I thought, *"Mr Tugey, I love you! You're the BEST! You've just made the cutest boy in class sit next to me as a punishment!"*

It wasn't long before Mr Tugey was rolling his eyes and saying in despair,

"Dani and Steven, if you don't stop talking, I am going to have to separate you!"

And the whole class fell about laughing and saying, *"Ooooh!"* as if we were in love!

To be honest, I did have a crush on Steven but normally, I would never sit next to him or show him that I liked him because I wasn't allowed. This was probably the first and last time I would ever get to sit next to my crush and it was all because of Mr Tugey!

I decided that day that he was the BEST teacher in the whole world and I couldn't wait for him to "punish" me again!

Chapter Seventeen- Culture Clash

Growing up between two totally different cultures is never easy. My parents came to Britain in the 1960s from a country called East Pakistan which used to be part of India. It's a whole other continent where the culture is different and the rules are so much stricter. So, I live in one continent and I have to behave as if I'm living in another!

Unlike my English friends who are free to fall in love, when a boy shows an interest in me, I have to look the other way even if I like him too. I have to keep my feelings all bottled up. I'm not allowed to fall in love and I'm not allowed to have a boyfriend so it can be a bit awkward when a boy asks me out.

The first time a boy asked me out was when I was ten. When he asked me out, a girl called Michelle from my class warned me,

"You can't say no to Rajesh Kelly. He's the most popular boy in school. If you say no to him, everyone is going to hate you!"

The first girl to say no to Rajesh had been Priti, one of the prettiest girls in the school. He'd asked her to marry him back in the second year when they were eight! When she'd said no, he had burst into tears and she felt so bad, she said,

"OK! OK! I'll marry you! STOP crying!"

He was so pleased when she said that she'd marry him that he gave her a black plastic ring that he'd got the Christmas before in a Christmas cracker! That was her engagement ring.

They stayed engaged until they were nine and then, they broke up and so, now, here he was a year later, at the age of ten, asking me out.

When he asked me if I'd go out with him, I remembered Michelle's warning and I was scared to say no to the most handsome, most popular boy in school.

So, when he asked me,

"Do you like me? Will you go out me?" I replied, *"Er... I'm not sure if I can go out with you. Can...can.. you give me some time to think it over?"*

And every time he asked me what I'd decided, I tried to stall him, saying,

"I need more time."

In the end, one day, he confronted me in the school playground and he said,

"I have to know NOW. Do you like me? Will you go out with me?"

I was scared to turn down the most popular boy in school, so I said,

"I really, really, really, really, really, REALLY like you but I can't go out with you. I'm sorry. I'm really sorry."

Rajesh was not impressed.

"Why didn't you tell me this before?"

"I didn't want to hurt your feelings," I said sheepishly.

"Well, you've hurt me now!" he cried before stomping off, furious with me for stalling him for so long!

I was afraid that everyone would hate me but luckily, ten-year-old hearts heal fast and a couple of weeks later, he fell in love with another girl so I was off the hook!

Now, two years later, I found another cute and popular boy asking me out, a girl who wasn't allowed to date or to look at a boy because of religion and because of culture, so what I was going to do?

This time the boy in question was Daxton Blair, one of the cutest boys in school who was part of a really cool group of kids who could break dance! How could I say no?

Daxton hangs out in a group of twelve boys who call themselves the Whizzkids and I hang out in a group of four girls who call themselves the Whizkids! Every week, we have a secret Whizkids meeting where we try to solve mysteries and save the world but the only mystery we have found so far and have been discussing has been,

"Is Miss Yianni dating Mr Reid and if so, how can we know?"

We keep looking for mysteries to solve like Nancy Drew but nothing mysterious ever happens at our school!

Well, anyway, I noticed that Daxton and his friends kept looking over at me and my friends and I thought that he liked my friend, Shilpa because she's the prettiest in our group even though she wears glasses.

Imagine my surprise when my friend, Paulami, and I were walking along a corridor in the school and Conal, a smallish boy with floppy blondish, brownish hair yelled out,

"Oi you! My mate fancies you!" to me!

He was pointing at Daxton who was leaning by a window opposite a classroom, looking cool and as Paulami and I walked past him, he looked straight at me and smiled and said, *"I do you know."*

I nearly died! Paulami and I looked at each other as if to say,

"WHAT just happened here?"

I couldn't believe what had happened!

Daxton Blair, one of the cutest and coolest boys in the school had just told me that he liked me, little me with my pigtails who was a boffin and who was definitely not cool!

I was the girl who had failed horribly when she had tried to do the splits in mid-air and had to go hopping to the other side of the road to get her shoe!

I can't breakdance. I can't spin on my head! I can't even do a handstand!

WHY would he like ME? I was so stunned that I walked by in shock without saying a word!

Plus, there was nothing I could do. What could I tell him?

"Daxton, my mother thinks that I am still a little kid and doesn't let me out with boys. In fact, I'm never allowed to have a boyfriend ever. It's against the rules."

My mum says that "good girls" don't have boyfriends, that no one will marry you if you have a boyfriend. They'll say,

"This is a bad girl. She had a boyfriend!"

She says,

"If you have a boyfriend, people will say that you're a bad girl and no one will ever marry you. You'll end up alone. Do you want to end up alone?"

I'm so scared of ending up alone with no husband and no children after having no father and no brothers and sisters that I say no to every boy who asks me out! I don't want to end up alone. I don't want to end up with less again, a second time!

Chapter Eighteen- "Hope"

Money is tight at home so we can't afford anything more than just the basics.

Sometimes, I feel that I'm just existing and not living as life is all about homework, housework and chores most of the time because we have no money to have fun or to do nice things.

My mother doesn't get any child support so, there are no violin or dance lessons for me!

We can't afford holidays. I've never even learned to ride a bike because Mum won't let me out to play on the estate with the other kids because she says it's too dangerous. She probably couldn't spend money on a luxury like a bike any way because money is so tight.

So, I just watch the kids from my school riding their BMX bikes around the estate from my window and I wish I could join in with them but I can't, so I do my homework and the housework and endless chores and wait and hope and pray for the day when life gets better, for the day when life isn't endless monotony anymore because we're poor.

My mother tries to cheer me up by taking me to the library every week to borrow books because she says it's important to read books and not just sit there gawping at a TV screen for hours at a time. So, I've read Roots by Alex Haley and now, I'm reading Greek myths and legends.

I like the story about Persephone and her mother, Demeter. They're a single parent family like me and my mother, just one parent and one child, a mother and a daughter. That's like my life! The bond between a single parent and her only child is intense because you've only got each other. That other person is your whole world so I can understand why Demeter went into mourning when she lost Persephone to Hades. I can't imagine how I'd cope if I ever lost my mother.

Right now, I've just finished reading another Greek story about Pandora, a really curious girl who was given a box and was told never ever to open the box but to keep it shut forever but Pandora let her curiosity get the better of her. She opened the box and all kinds of evil things flew out of that box and into the world, things like jealousy, envy, anger and greed.

But after all kinds of evil things came flying out of that box, there was ONE good thing that came out and that was HOPE.

My mother says that we have to keep hope no matter how tough life gets. She says that when I'm sixteen and in sixth form, she's going to go back to work and she's going to be a teacher again just like she used to be in her own country.

She's not working now because we live on a rough council estate so she walks me to and from school to make sure that I'm safe and because she doesn't want me to fall in with the wrong crowd at high school and become a latch-key kid!

My mum says that if I'm good and if I work hard and follow the rules, I am going to have a great life. She still says,

"If at first, you don't succeed, try, try again!" just like she did when I was seven when she made me do the verbal test a second time after I had failed the first time !

My mother was right. I did pass the second time because I tried again!

She also says that we have to keep going and we have to keep doing what's right and holding onto hope even when life is tough. My mum says,

"God tests the ones he loves!"

So, even when life feels like endless monotony, endless rounds of housework and homework and endless chores, I comfort myself with the promise that it won't always be this way.

I tell myself that things will get better someday.

If I follow the rules, work hard and do all the right things like my mother says, someday, life will be better than this. I won't be just existing because of poverty. I will be living!

So, when life feels like a tragedy and when I feel like giving up, I remind myself that the best is yet to come.

I remind myself of my mother's words,

"If you trust in God and do what's right, there is always hope."

I remind myself of that every day.

There is always hope.

Printed in Great Britain
by Amazon

47697815R00056